Shadows Set to Burn
poems

Shadows Set to Burn
poems

Linda Flaherty Haltmaier

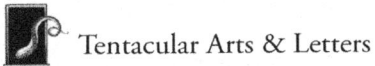
Tentacular Arts & Letters

Tentacular Arts & Letters
Boston, Massachusetts
www.tentaculararts.com

© 2024 • Text by Linda Flaherty Haltmaier
All rights reserved. Except for brief quotations in critical articles or reviews, no part of this book may be reproduced without prior written permission from the publisher.

Published in 2024 • Tentacular Arts & Letters
Cover and Interior Designed by RBH Design
Cover Image: Karl Friedrich Thiele, *Design for The Magic Flute: The Hall of Stars in the Palace of the Queen of the Night, Act 1, Scene 6,* 1847

ISBN • 978-1-7374372-7-7

ALSO BY THE AUTHOR

Catch and Release

...

Rolling up the Sky
Winner of the Homebound Publications
Poetry Prize

...

To the Left of the Sun
Winner of the International Book Award
for Poetry

For Rick & Rory, my true loves.

&

For Brenna & Dick, whose passions live on in me today.

Table of Contents

Epigraph: Creation Story

I. In the Marrow

3   A Visitation at Dinner
5   Vows
6   The Sound of Two Hands Touching
8   Untended/Unintended
9   Party Dress
10 Mathematics and Motherhood
12 The Darkness of a Father
14 Love Unbridled
16 A Spider Named Number 16
18 Original Sin
19 Cartwheeling into Joy
20 *Pater Familias*
21 Wire Monkey

II. Waiting for Sleep

24 Incoming
25 The Underpainting
27 Out of her mind today
28 A Time for Euphemisms
29 Just Rest Your Bones
30 Moving to the Uncanny Valley
32 In the Kitchen of Grief
33 Three Weeks After the Funeral
34 Rest Here
36 Calender Interrupted
37 Baker's Secret

III. Cantilevered Hope

40 A Moment
41 Darkness, looming
43 Instinct
44 Uneasy Truce
46 Know This
48 Grit
49 Combustible Women
50 When will the time be right?
51 Demolition
52 Downpour
53 Morning Fix

IV. Stretching into Light

56 To the Brink
58 Speaking Lilac
59 Ode to a Cornichon
60 Bibliophile's Daughter
62 Ordinary Divine
64 The Humanity of Knees
65 The Beaten-down of Boca Raton
66 Furrow Meet Botox
67 The Watcher
68 The Muses
69 Broken Open
70 Museum of the Ordinary
72 The Profligate Universe

Acknowledgements
With Gratitude
About the Author

In order to give light
one must first burn.

—Rumi

Creation Story

Not all poetry is created
in a place that glimmers
like the halls of Versailles
or smells like cognac
and musty pages held tight
by the spines of the masters.
Some poetry is born
in that place out back
where old things,
forgotten things,
rusty, pointed things
that cut jagged and deep
get tossed,
ones that demand a tetanus
shot and too much gauze.
It's there
where poems first mewl—
alone,
in the dark,
behind a door outlined in flame.

In the Marrow

A Visitation at Dinner

It has been a while
since the gash in the ground
swallowed my mother,
her brass and mahogany chariot
slipped beneath the feet of the living
and the crying,
each cradling a lily plucked in silence,
a starburst of remembrance
sanctified by the moment.

Life hurried on,
gained speed,
her funeral card dropped into
the drawer of confusing objects,
cousin to the junk drawer,
where locks of baby hair, defunct keychains,
and collars of pets long passed
are stashed and pushed about,
their value utterly worthless
yet incalculable—
the paradox of what is left behind.

But somehow my mother showed up
at dinner the other night
between sips of Cabernet
and knowing laughs with friends.
Slipped the bolt
from the other side
and waved me through
to a place where grace grows

like the pinkest phlox in May,
redolent and lush.

And as if sprinkled with
the forgetting waters of Lethe,
I felt my armored heart tilt
toward curiosity,
filled with a fondness
for the person she was
and tried to be,
wondering about the origin story
of the freckled redhead
who loved to play stickball
with the boys.

How this visitation occurred is unclear—
perhaps an undigested bit of beef
or a strange alchemy of time, distance,
and red wine—
but something softened that night,
rage gone slack,
a respite.

Stripped of my bespoke grievances,
I could see her beyond the threshold,
perhaps the way God sees us—
flawed and fallible,
worthy of love,
swinging full tilt
at both balls and strikes.

Vows

I am stitched into your skin
and you into mine,
the reds and blues
of my veins
and arteries
wrap around you
in a skein of tangles
like garter snakes locked
in a ball of creation—
a quivering manifestation
of hope vying for infinity,
a Gordian knot
of me and you,
sinew and promise.

The Sound of Two Hands Touching

The priest sleepwalks
through a send off
for a man you and I loved
in decidedly different measure—
your husband, my father.

You reach for my hand,
drift-wood fingers tap across the pew,
a dazed tarantula at daybreak,
sensing body heat.

Then a metallic shriek on contact,
a vertebral groan,
sounds of a Baltic shipyard
as discs lock one onto the other—
my spine a frozen zipper,
finding its slot at my throat.

Kidneys, heart, lungs
all stand down
as sensation pours
into nerve endings,
this hand on mine,
mother and daughter,
flesh on flesh—

I've seen snapshots of you
holding me as a baby,
still, the urge to pull away,
primal,
overwhelming.

Only fragments of the funeral remain,
censers of incense
swing in hypnotic rhythm
as smoke and lamentations
mingle skyward—

And knuckles, swollen
and familiar,
rest on my fingers
like a bronze cast of hands
I once saw in a catalogue.

Untended/Unintended

Not sure why my sister's hair did that, grew out of her head like twisted, wild vines. Some spirals were as taut as coils in a ripped mattress I once saw in the woods with beer cans strewn all around. I felt a strange chill there, like something terrible might have happened. Her curls reminded me of lollipops the tattooed carnies hawked when they rolled into town every June—a rainbow on a stick. A dagger of swirled sugar in crayon colors. I'd beg for one and on first lick, I'd remember the double-cross—it tasted like old paste. Like disappointment all dressed up. The last time, I smashed it on the asphalt and watched it shatter like a frozen firework. Mom used to say that a girl's hair is her fortune. Maybe that's why she'd wrap my hair in tie-dyed rags before bed and once gave me a home perm in the kitchen sink. The burning scalp was nearly worth it— for one shining moment I had a bouncy fortune on my head. Until the curls fell out after kickball and I was a drowned rat again. "Hair out of your face," she'd say, flicking a limp strand from my cheek. My sister's hair was a tangled mess and mine a handful of milkweed fluff after a rainstorm. Until the day my sister discovered the power of a blow-dryer. She lingered at the mirror longer than any fairy princess or evil queen, learned how to tame those tangles, spun them into gold like Rumpelstiltskin with a round brush. Feathered those wires to a sleek auburn gloss with flecks of honey. And it changed everything. She saved up for Calvin Kleins, learned eye make-up from a magazine, and soon was out to the woods with the boys and the beer. Out to the place with the mattress. Mom smiled at her like she was belle of the ball.

Party Dress

Black velvet tiers,
a wearable birthday cake—
if I spun fast enough,
each layer would rise,
the lift off, a muffled sound
like baby crows learning to fly.
A satin ribbon circled my waist
with a rose bigger than a doll's head—
it bobbed
and flopped
as I skipped along
the gravel edge of the road.
Mary Janes scrape sandy pavement,
a favorite sound—
harbinger of frosting, balloons,
and tiny wooden paddles
to scoop the yin/yang divide
between chocolate and vanilla.

Mathematics and Motherhood

A degree in math and physics,
no calculus problem too complex,
the elliptical orbits of Mars and Neptune
within grasp,
the laws of the universe–
gravity,
force,
velocity,
no mystery to her.

Cherry-picked to grapple
with the first computers
in a time when women were
presumed too preoccupied
with mascara and kitten heels
to give Archimedes and Newton
much thought.

I imagine her with the Rubik's Cube
she never got to solving:
the red of Dad's fingers
digging into tiny arms,
the yellow and green of fading marks,
the orange of the kitchen rug
as he thundered,
the blue and white pinstripe
of his shirt
untucked from exertion.

Did she hold this puzzle
in her hands,
turn it over and around,
wrestle with it for our sake,
struggling to line up the rows?

We waited for her
to come up with the answer—
the solution
always the null set.

The Darkness of a Father

I give it back to him,
it was never mine anyway,
a gift not found under a Christmas tree
or next to a birthday cake
but one handed over in chaotic moments
witnessed by a child.

A darkness that flowered in anger
and frustration,
fueled by the loss of a mother,
black and white snapshots captured
her radiant Irish face—
a Galway County beauty
with a crooked smile that
found its way to the curve of his lips.

A boy of five doesn't know
how to say goodbye—
How many nights did he ask for her?
And how did the grief-stricken answer?
Their voices stolen by harpies,
her name carried off to the land of forgetting,
a memory of obliteration—
stricken from the record,
never to be mentioned again.

Later he donned the robes of a novitiate
to wrap himself in the arms of God
but solace was elusive
and final vows
stillborn in his mouth.

A wound that never knit,
no salve strong enough
to take away the pain—
it lived in the bones of our house,
in the marrow of our family,
an animal as alive
as the dog under the table
begging for scraps.

Love Unbridled

Troika bounds towards me
as the bus pulls away,
a missile of fur and tongue and glee—
I hold out my book bag
to body block all the love coming at me.

She chaperones me down Solon Street,
so named for the ruler that codified Roman laws—
but this tail-wagging centurion's only law
a simple conflation of food and love.

It's any day in late April,
drizzly and slick,
sun on cue for a late afternoon cameo.
I stop at a neighbor's colossal lilac bush
laden with drunk blooms.
I twist and twirl a knotty stem,
ombre blossoms flaring—
wrestle the stubborn flourish
to a jarring decapitation.

I carry this offering into the kitchen
and present it to my mother
as if it were Medusa's freshly lopped head—
my eyes and attention now transfixed
by the heaps of cookies
cooling on wire racks.

The sight of molten chocolate
washes away any worries
a fifth grader may keep close—
I become one with a warm golden disc,

tipsy from the scent of caramelized sugar
and unable to remember how my day was
until at least the second bite.

Mom slips the lilacs into a Mason jar
and awaits my return
at a sink full of suds.

A Spider Named Number 16

Beneath the Acacia tree
in remotest Australia,
a newborn nobody holes up
in a woven sac of silk,
sealed beneath a trapdoor—
a tell-tale spiral of needles
spins from its locus,
a circular door with a hidden hinge.

Her mother left her
in this underground desert hideout
with the other spiderlings,
to be awakened by hunger and instinct,
to find their way in the world,
to build their own tidy trapdoor homes,
to lie in wait until vibrations
alert them to burst out
and feast on the unsuspecting.

She journeyed nearly six feet to make
her silken burrow, a home for one.
Venturing out only for meals
or to weave a Valentine for suitors,
a doily lace banner for her door,
signaling her openness
to their attentions—
the imperative to procreate
hard-wired
into even the most solitary.

A zoologist with a passion
for arachnids discovered her, the Acacia,
and its band of subterranean dwellers.
An updated Miss Muffet,
Barbara York Main placed
a "Number 16" medallion by this spider's front door
and visited her eight-legged subjects
for decades—
studied their progress,
charted their triumphs and demises,
celebrated their resilience—
a brutal existence on a barren patch of scrub
for creatures no bigger than a nickel.

She came back for forty-three years
until too frail for the journey,
passed the torch to a colleague
who found Number 16's door ripped off its hinges,
pristine spiral smashed—
a predatory wasp
had broken into her lair
and cornered its meal.

A legacy of grit documented over four decades—
Number 16 remains the oldest spider
in recorded history.
Mother to thousands of trapdoor spiderlings,
she made a life in a cruel landscape,
a solitary survivor
watched over by a loyal scientist,
a master class in shared tenacity.

Original Sin

You stood by,
watched the rage build,
heard him pushing into her room
as locked knees strained
to keep him out.

She called your name over and over—
Mom with too many o's,
vowel held like Maria Callas in her prime,
this solo for your ears alone.

Unimpressed, you flipped a page
in *House Beautiful* magazine
and dreamed of redecorating
the living room in brown velvet.

Cartwheeling into Joy

My cartwheels were never textbook
twirls of hands over feet,
stretching toes
and starfish perfection.

Mine were more crumpled arachnid
in final death throes,
limbs comically akimbo—
much to the delight of my sisters
who lorded their stretchy-legged
and pointy-toed superiority
over me.

Still, it was worth their ridicule
to feel grass digging into palms
on a wide-open summer day—
the faint scent of earthworms
inches from my nose,
determined sweat sputniking
as legs launch into the eggy blue
with a flutter kick of upside-down hope—
their peals of laughter
atomizing in my skull
as I dared to find
my place among the clouds.

Pater Familias

My head tangled in a pajama top,
the bedroom door flies open,
he stands, hand on knob
watching chaos and exposed flesh
as I shriek and cover up.

It doesn't happen once or twice
or fifty times
but enough to turn me
into a Comanche warrior,
footfalls and creaky floorboards

alive at twenty paces.
I lie in wait for the interloper
as I conjugate Latin verbs,
tell secrets to my diary,
sketch bluebirds and manta rays.

I block the door a millisecond late
one time and wrench my wrist—
I stuff a sock in the door
from then on,
slamming it in tight

so it can't fling open—
a quarter inch
of polyester/cotton blend
separating me
from a relentless imp.

Wire Monkey

I hear women say
that their mother is their best friend—
and I marvel at the thought.
A beautiful, incomprehensible thought,
like spotting a horseshoe crab
at low tide for the very first time.

My mom and I sit at a linen draped table,
just the two of us
overlooking the gush and swirl of morning
on Boston's Newbury Street.
I'm twenty years old and away at college—
I say that I wish that we could be friends,
somehow melt the iciness between us.

She reaches for a piece of charred rye
slotted in the ribs of a silver rack—
"I'm your mother.
I have no interest in being your friend."
Butter scrapes toast,
a knife plunges into jam.

Moments like this one,
stinging in their before-and-after clarity,
linger like red wine on a white rug.
A ghost of something
gone terribly wrong remains,
despite all efforts to scrub it away—
an emotional crime scene
without the yellow tape.

I think of the baby monkeys
in Harlow's famous experiment
we learned about in psychology class—

separated from their mothers forever,
left clinging to a wire monkey
covered with a blanket,
a pitiful stand-in for a mother—
no amount of wishing
or hugging
would ever make her real.

Waiting for Sleep

Incoming

My mother is a sandcastle,
dementia the tide,
merciless,
unrelenting,
wearing down the edges,
eroding the essential her-ness
that gave her shape—
memories, likes, dislikes,
grains of identity returning to the sea.
The tide takes her favorite color,
her love of fashion,
the lace-curtain Irish humor that bit hard,
the names of her children.

The Underpainting

She was the too-busy blur,
the always-moving mother of five,
little time for anything but the basics:
Don't forget your hat.
Finish your broccoli.
Time to hit blanket street.

Then dementia sent in termites
to nibble away at the edges,
bathing her mind in turpentine,
the veneer of social civility thinned,
stripping layers of pretense,
revealing the original brushstrokes
of the woman beneath—

An underpainting in vermilion red,
cadmium yellow,
vibrancy laid bare—
a creamy highlight on kindness,
an ochre flick of laughter,
a dab of carnation pink in the shadows.

Her Jamaican aides get the best of her now,
this colorful, untethered woman
who razzes them
about hairstyles and fuchsia lipstick—
all that's left of this fading world,
a frothy, ping-pong banter we never shared—

I feel a distant pang of jealousy,
a sense of dislocation as I watch them.

Her eyes tell me that
I'm a stranger again today.
I call her Mom a few times
and gravity is restored—

I am your daughter and
you are my mother,
and I'll do my best to visit
with a woman I'm not sure
I ever really knew.

Out of her mind today

The prognosis,
not given by an actual doctor
but my sister
who parked my mother
in an exercise class at the dementia ward,
secured the wheelchair,

and fled as though locusts were
swarming Egypt—
into light and air,
away from the stale reek
of the warehoused.

Every Sunday at mass,
the priest told us to pray
for the shut-ins.
I mumbled the prayer
but had no idea who they were
or why they'd been shut in.

Sometimes they would creep
into my thoughts at bedtime,
fresh from a Hieronymus Bosch hellscape—
the ramp to sleep blocked
by this secret worry.

Poor trapped souls
worthy of prayer
but not escape.
I always wondered why
nobody ever let them out.

A Time for Euphemisms

When the time draws near
and turkey vultures
sniff out their next meal,
certain words disappear
from the lexicon:
death
dying
dead
all jettisoned for their softer cousins—
transitioning,
letting go,
passing on.
Maybe it's the D sound
that hits too hard—
like the klonk of a hammer.
It's fine for *dog* and *dandelion*
but dead has a "d" on either end
and a sigh in the middle.
Dead.
Thud, sigh, thud.

Just Rest Your Bones

These, the last words I say to my mother,
her face unlined as a kewpie doll,
once bee-stung lips stretched colorless,
an inadvertent Munch portrait,
breaths halting.

My sisters told her it was okay to go,
Dad was waiting—
but I floundered,
flubbed that simple line.

Instead, I found myself
repeating a mantra
she'd whisper to me on hot nights
when I had trouble sleeping—
the air still and moist,
no fan to ease the swelter.

She'd run a wet cloth
over my arms and legs,
and finally my face.
Just rest your bones, she'd say
so close to my ear it tickled—
and I'd lie there, grateful,
a limp starfish,
waiting for sleep
to carry me away.

Moving to the Uncanny Valley

In the blur of days
that followed your exit,
to universes unknown and
never knowable,
I sensed my atoms rearranging,
cascading into place
like the departure board
at Penn Station,
clacking furiously to adjust
to this updated time and track
without you.

This new formulation of me,
not so different on the outside
but for plummy half-moons
won in a fistfight with death,
and my ability to stare
into the middle distance indefinitely,
lost in a murky aquarium of memory—

a husk self that can make tea,
put on a black dress,
and nod appropriately.
An approximation of me,
not the one that existed
when you were here,
the parts steeped
in decades of us
now starved for your essence.

Physicists say that atoms observed
behave differently
than those not watched,
the very act of being observed
changes them.
So what happens when the gaze is gone?

It's too soon to tell
but one day I'll report back from
the uncanny valley
where I and the rest of the
gutted, bereaved, and forlorn
pantomime through daily life,
grocery shopping and chit chatting
like normal people,
knowing that we are forever altered
and rearranged
under these flimsy flesh coverings.

In the Kitchen of Grief

My body is grieving
but my mind is staying out of it.
I binge on endless baking shows—

Hands knead dough,
meringue whips into glossy peaks,
buttercream frosts the earth,
and unacknowledged tears
stream from the corners of my eyes
as if I'd sprung a leak.

My mother is gone
and my body knows what to do.
She loved me with brownies, snickerdoodles
and gooey Congo squares.
Sweets, not sweet nothings, her forte.

I bake her chocolate cake
in the dented pan she used for eons,
once her mother's,
a relic so worn and tarnished
I'm not sure the batter will hold.

The smell of warm cocoa fills the house,
seeps into the slammed shut spaces,
the walled off corners—
nibbling at the deep freeze
of a heart nudged into early thaw.

Tears come now,
ripples of grief
in watery lock step
with every bite.

Three Weeks After the Funeral

The flowers droop,
nearly decapitated.
Browning faces,
slack necks.
The water, a swamp,
the stench of rot settling in.
They can stay a while longer.

Rest Here

Without us,
the bumblebee still sputters
to the rhododendron,
Saturn slings in its orbit,
and morning glories blink purple
at twilight.

Without us,
sea turtle hatchlings
scramble into the brine undeterred,
while leaves of the magnolia
turn sunlight into sugar
and sugar into expectant buds.

Without us,
the universe carries on,
finds its way.

So rest here awhile,
put away your worries,
your dread,
make a pillow from your jacket
and lean into the cool grass—
the world is teeming
with unseen rhythms and magic
that have no need of you right now.

Rest here
and fill your lungs with
the possibility of just
this moment—

to be held by the earth
and tickled by the dandelions,
as clouds stand guard
and the thinnest circle of moon
washes onto a benevolent sky.

Calendar Interrupted

And so it is today, again.
The days once so important
with their august names,
tributes to the moon and sun
and select, anointed planets,
are lost to me now.

The rhythm of night to day
and day to night
metronomes
reliable and sure—
nature's trains do run on time.

And so it is today, again,
I think as I wake,
the trail to the coffee pot
offering no clues along the way.

Maybe the house finch
beyond the kitchen window
has a hunch.
Perhaps Thursdays
are for fetching dried grass
and Tuesdays are meant for love.

Or maybe that clump of daffodils
straining as if to hear a secret,
might know the day,
the sun's fingerlings
tantalizing and near.
I sense the damp earth knows
but won't say.
And so it is today, again.

Baker's Secret

I meet you in the space of memory now,
archived moments
safe from actual togetherness
yet tinged
with asynchronous affection.

I think of the lemon scone you loved,
the one from the bakery in Cambridge
near Julia Child's house.
I discovered it too,
independent of you—
stalked it often,
broke pieces off the fist-sized lump,
a human heart of flour, butter, and zest,
gaudy with thick glaze.
It demanded two cups of coffee
just to make a dent.

Dad walked in with your lemon scone one day—
our shared obsession laid bare.
You too, had fallen under its sweet spell.
Even so, our magnetic north never lined up—
I made your needle spin wildly.

Talking was hard,
more than mother-daughter hard.
A bolt of panic crackled
whenever you found yourself alone with me.
What might spill out of that mouth?
your eyes seemed to say.

But we could talk lemon scones
and blueberry muffins with a sugary dome

like the ones from Jordan Marsh—
or the triumphant *île flottante* you made
for your tennis lunch.

Sometimes I dream of those floating islands,
pillowy quenelles drifting
on a custard lake—
there in a landscape of whipped eggs and sugar,
we found common ground.

Cantilevered Hope

A Moment

Change doesn't arrive
with a brass band and streamers—
it shows up as the low hum of the soul,
breaking through in a moment of quiet.

Enough, enough, it says
in the gentle way we speak to children,
full of kindness and empathy.
It's time.

And you will know what that means
as the message seeps into the spaces
that couldn't receive it before—
floods them with resolve,
sticky and lasting,
like honey finding its chamber.

Darkness, looming

My tricks are failing,
the ways I dull and distract myself
from the abyss.
I dangle on the edge,
kicking for a tree branch
to appear underfoot,
jutting out like cantilevered hope.

This time I find myself
at the bottom of a canyon
under a three A.M. squid ink sky,
stumbling by cacti with
arms outstretched—
an anxious, loping mummy
tempting a scorpion's paintbrush poison tip
or the taut nerves
of a trapdoor spider.

Better to sit and meld with the darkness,
let the night creatures skitter and slink
under stars that blaze beyond
the prickly pears—
a pincushion dome of light
born before amoebas ruled the earth,
beaming now for me.

The thought clicks open a
spaciousness inside,
like a skeleton key opening
a door to a secret room—
and on the other side
there is coffee and Cabernet,

cherry-capped woodpeckers
and dozing otters,
someone to ask about my day,
someone who knows my darkness
and stays anyway.

The first slit of daybreak
flares Aztec gold
at the horizon,
shadows set to burn.

Instinct

The skin around your leaving
won't knit—
defiant edges
await your return,
raw and ready,
but time has swallowed you,
returned you to the deep—

To join newborn cephalopods
whose tiny transparent hearts
throb like a bruise.

To dodge anglerfish
that dangle their glowing bulb,
an errant book light
bobbing for the curious
and the doomed.

To join leatherbacks
with an instinct for moonlight—
the longitude of loss
a missing strand
on their double helix.

They find their way home,
always,
certain that someone
or something
waits there just for them.

Uneasy Truce

Shall I lay my weapon down,
just for a spell,
slam it on the table
like a cowboy
in need of a stiff drink?

This weapon doesn't
glint in the sun or
make a satisfying thud—
it's holstered to the underside
of my ribs,
wedged in by my heart
where the battle tools are kept.

A cache of silver bullets
engraved with my failings,
hand grenades that explode
with criticism for acts great and small,
a collection of rusty knives,
curved and serrated,
for cutting out disappointments
and failures too hard to bear.

Get too cocky and there's
a cherry bomb to choke me
out of my arrogance,
feeling pretty good in those new jeans,
here's a karate chop
to the solar plexus.

And ten thousand volts await
the thought that maybe
there's another way,
a better way
to move in the direction of my dreams.

The arsenal stocked,
the trigger slick against my finger—
but more often now,
the white flag flutters
like petals of a daisy
caught in a breeze
on a too-hot day—
daring my sweaty grip to hold,
beckoning for a truce.

Know This

This is what you must know,
the secret tattooed
on the flank of your soul—
You belong here.

You are as essential as a basset hound
dozing on a spot of sunshine,
as lovable as a sea otter
floating in the harbor,
as worthy as the purple asters
in the garden,
their mouths open in permanent wonder—
and as necessary as the dragonflies
that visit them.

You belong here,
on planet Earth,
right here, right now.

Your value is fixed like the North Star
and does not rise and fall
like the price of gold.

Mistakes, setbacks, grand mess-ups
paint a heart with the patina of the brave—
a sheen earned from a life
of testing your powers
whatever they may be—
to take chances,
unclench your heart,
fail and succeed with equal grace.

There's no rent to be paid for your being here—
whether or not
you catch the fly ball,
land the dream job,
or write the next *Hamlet*.

You belong
here,
just as you are,
in all your glorious imperfection.

Grit

To tread on a piece of forever,
to feel the gritty residue underfoot,
boulders fragmented over eons,
supernovae exploding
in slow motion,
one beautiful thing
begetting another.

The eloquent violence
of the ocean
grinding down,
making way,
the moon whispering
the tides back and forth.

Tiny fragments
of mountain, juniper,
spiny crustacean,
a world in miniature—
the squeak and grit
of transformation,
one step
then another,
a never-ending cycle
of rebirth—
hope lodged between my toes.

Combustible Women

I want us to inhabit our bodies
the way plutonium inhabits
a nuclear warhead.

I want us to occupy our skin
like sunbathing grandmothers
on the Cote d'Azur,
flaunting their terra cotta curves,
shoulders squared
against a beating sun,
topless and unabashed.

I want us to stop saying
"You look great, have you lost weight?"
when we greet each other,
as if the shape of our bodies
is the one newsworthy topic.

I want us to celebrate these
imperfect,
maligned,
and magnificent bodies
for all that they do
without fanfare or recognition—

To celebrate the miracle
of each breath,
the persistence
of this pounding heart,
the Technicolor world
streaming through our eyes.

When will the time be right?

Bound up in a chrysalis,
drowning in the becoming
but never quite becoming,
nourishing liquid
turns rancid,
all the preparation
a stalling tactic.

Maybe my wings aren't pretty enough,
strong enough,
shaped just so.
I might look ridiculous,
come out too early or too late—
they might laugh.
Thoughts that keep us soaking
in cozy stasis—

but the Monarch
is wired for freedom
and the skies,
transformation not complete
until her damp wings,
fibrillating from effort
and exhaustion,
feel the urgent breeze
against them.

She'll die
if helped from her pod,
the struggle to break free
the very thing
that makes her able to fly.

Demolition

I want to invite
tenderness
and spaciousness
into my life.

These walls
of cracked mortar
and brick-fired shame,
stacked by the hands of a child,

protected the soft belly,
the innocence curdling
in silence,
walling off the chaos.

Now a blight
to the gentrifying neighborhood,
the boogeyman long since
moved away,

walls meant to protect
now isolate.
A shove or two,
a pinwheel of determined kicks

could bring the wall down,
unleash the *yes*
of one who sees freedom
on the other side.

Downpour

A tarnished sterling sky
bears down on the day
like a toddler with a crayon,
determined to make its mark.

A first tap on the shoulder,
then elbow, ankle,
droplets dive-bomb mid-stride.
I squirrel-step now,
sneakers squeak and caw
at the uptick.

I duck under a Jurassic bush,
its canopy of Medusa tendrils,
sturdy, wild, elegant,
a Martha Graham among trees—
outcroppings of paddle-shaped
leaves deflect and intervene,
shielding my straw hat.

Last night's puddles
ping and ploof
in ruts by the road,
Mondrian-ing a riff of circles—
murky pools a canvas
of interlocking rings,
a mandala in hydrogen and oxygen,
there then gone—

I hold my breath,
a sneakered monk
contemplating impermanence.

Morning Fix

I eat Sylvia Plath for breakfast,
between bites of toast,
burnt edges
raining soot on the page,
a *linea nigra* forming
in the belly of the book,
a pregnancy of words.

Her *red tulips* and *bright needles*
eclipse my other senses,
and the toast,
even the jam,
have no taste—
stanzas fill my mouth,
crowd my teeth,
my tongue a limp, stunned animal.

Images race down my arms and legs
on tracks the addict treads,
highways of *chi* in full flame,
pricking knots of ganglia
and unsuspecting toes
with wonder
and heartache.

Stretching into Light

To the Brink

If it is to be
that I end up in a box,
primped and propped,
lips stretched into a Modigliani slash,
while lilies, sickly sweet,
mask the true visitor
in the corner—

Then get me to the ocean,
the carnival,
the park,
the Eiffel Tower,
the farmer's market full
of sweet potato pies
and jams I've never tasted.

Get me to fresh air and dirt,
to dig cozy spots for bulbs
that burst with the promise
of tangerine and fuchsia,
even as spring plays
its deadly hide-and-seek.

Get me to the page,
where I can capture
my daughter's face as she draws,
her determined tongue locked in,
or the way my husband
looks at her sometimes,
punch-drunk with pride and love.

Take me to the brink of exhaustion,
my head bursting
with color and awe,
a sunflower at full glow,
love spilling out of me
like hard black seeds
onto welcoming ground.

Speaking Lilac

Capturing the ineffable
is like trying to catch a minnow.
You approach, determined to
scoop it in your hands—
it's right there, easy pickings,
the sleek, tiny body
an Art Deco wonder.
A metallic flash and it's gone—
no ripple to announce that it
had ever been there.
Like a moment
of divine contact
when the wisdom
of the squirrel
or lilac
or toadstool
reveals itself so clearly
that you speak lilac
or squirrel
or toadstool for an instant—
and by the next footfall,
the trail of silver knowing is lost.

Ode to a Cornichon

A tiny pickle with a French accent,
petite in size,
grand in punch,
a time machine powered by vinegar.

A crunch off the top and
I'm cross-legged on a bench
in the Tuileries,
a lull in solo travels across Europe,
only a backpack to my name.

Irises, poppies, and gladiolas
flutter for attention,
marble statues pose and flex,
and little girls too young for school
dart past in red shoes,
ponytails swishing.

One day I will have a little girl
in red shoes, I vow,
and we'll dash through
these gardens together,
hand in hand,
laughing,
kicking up sand behind us,
eyes fixed on the swing set ahead.

Bibliophile's Daughter

Books left on the bed,
his favorites for her to discover,
to discuss on rides out
for Bailey's hot fudge sundaes—
like finding a ticket
to ancient Egypt or the red planet
every other week.

A novel by the Czech author
who coined the word robot and
imagined a world of sentient newts
kicked off a love affair
with science fiction.
Soon H. Rider Haggard, Jules Verne,
and H.G. Wells
found a spot on her flowered bedspread,
delivered with hope,
received with anticipation.

The Time Machine was a hundred page
bite-sized read,
perfect for a fourth grader.
A Victorian man in purple velvet
looked dapper and desperate
on its cover—
she tore into yellowing pages
and by morning,
a stomachache that could only be cured
by a day of time travelling in bed.

Between bites of toast and
chicken noodle soup,
she devoured the adventures
of the time traveler and
his trouble with the Morlocks.

Her mom trundled in a rickety TV,
tin foil clumps festooned rabbit ears
once snapped in a forgotten fury—
but no soap opera
or showcase showdown
could ever compete with the
thrill of those words on the page.

Ordinary Divine

Anne Bradstreet was an unlikely first,
this newcomer to a colony across the Atlantic.
The land, untamed and unforgiving,
called with a promise of freedom—
worship at will, praise your God.
But the conventions and confinements
of society followed,
loaded in the hull of the *Arbella*,
ballast for a new ship of state.

An amphitheater of ancient voices
shaped her mind—
Virgil, Homer, Seneca, Milton—
she was educated full-bore like a son
when daughters were molded
for homebound duties.

Even in the brimstone reek
of the Massachusetts Bay Colony,
the woman's sphere could not contain her—
a mind teeming with erudition, science,
and philosophy.

Cloaked in the chaste trappings of her station,
she sought to make sense of the hardship
and sacrifice of her new home,
to plumb the mysteries of the ordinary divine—
scratching out verses that gave voice
to her struggles and passions,

mined her intellect and experience,
all while artfully maintaining a brood of eight,
a proper home, and the unassailable piety
of a Puritan wife.

Bradstreet's debut book of poems in 1650,
the first collection published
by a man or woman in America,
lauded for its sophistication and accessibility,
endures as a triumph of an unassuming spirit—
A titan at the kitchen table,
fingers blacked with ink,
determined to say her piece
despite the watchful eye
of her God and fellow man.

The Humanity of Knees

They're lined up on risers,
rapt and aglow,
girls in sundresses
entrained by a conductor's bow,
fledglings ready to take flight
at the down beat,
nearly-women teetering
on the edge—

I feel a pang at the exposed flesh,
the utter lack of guile—
these bare knees
that chug to class,
unleash soccer balls,
fly backwards over high bars,
once boo-boo kissed and
criss cross apple-sauced,

Now bear the weight of their future,
the burden of their femininity.
Each pair as distinct
as the girl it supports,
a phrenology of bumps
and shadows
crowned by a cotton frill.

The vulnerability
of bare limbs
stabs as the cantata
nears its crescendo.

The Beaten-down of Boca Raton

They carp orders,
shriveled royalty with cotton candy hair,
skin the color of worn Naugahyde
that hangs on them like King Lear's robes.

They wear the look of one caught
in a cloud of putrefaction,
a facial spasm of permanent disgust
with a lipstick gash that stretches
into a smile every odd Tuesday.

Their husbands
lope two steps behind in pairs,
bonded in servitude,
a life sentence decreed decades ago
when lust clouded a man's eyes—
bewitched by the way a girl
animated a pencil skirt
and sweater set.

They sealed their fate
with a diamond solitaire
and a prime rib reception.
Now they see their lot
with stinging clarity.
They hold purses and doors
in stooped silence,
listening to tales of cold soup
and air conditioning
that's never quite right.

Furrow Meet Botox

A needle jab right between the eyes,
the famous spot that bullets dream of hitting.
The burst on impact jolts,
braying nurses distract with gauze,
the sting of alcohol turns

the room into a watery collage—
She's a dazed Lepidoptera,
pricked and ready for cataloguing.
The doctor, with leading-man good looks
and a healthy dose of his own medicine,

speaks of poetry and a friend
who reads the classics over and over—
one hundred books on repeat,
Moby Dick, Pride & Prejudice,
To Kill a Mockingbird,

no room for a rogue title to break in,
no chance for new delights.
She clucks on cue and
presses gauze to her forehead,
against bubbles of poison

trapped beneath skin.
She glows under the surgical light,
a modern-day granny at the beauty parlor
waiting for her permanent to set,
inviting transformation.

The Watcher

Perhaps he straddles a seedling ball
in haze that shimmies off the muck,
skimming cattails,
dodging dragonflies intent on carnal delights—
an autumn pastoral pantomiming an eerie moor,
soon to be unmasked by sharp October rays.
Air shudders and rises,
a cubist painting disassembling
into pixels of liquid color.
Or perhaps he's a dragon beetle today,
the glint of molten emeralds on his wing casings,
watching with tiny television-screen eyes,
swiveling in wonder,
shaking his antennae.
They are magnificent,
my creations—
will they ever look up from their phones?

The Muses

Some say there were only three,
a triad of inspiration,
Hesiod tripled the crew to nine,
giving them jobs and names
like Calliope, Clio, and Erato—
amplifying the whispers
heard by mortals
that toil in the tar pits of creation.

I imagine them as mirrored figures,
nearly invisible,
that slip in and out of blind spots,
leaving trails of light behind—

A murmur under a dented hat
and Whitman sings a song of himself,
the notion to tell the truth, but slant,
lights on Emily at her bedroom window,
a visit to Eliot's London flat
ends with a bang not a whimper.

And eons before, a throaty hint
enshrines Odysseus's journey
to lands where pig men prosper
and women sing with tongues
of steel and promise.

Words strung together,
a godliness reflected back
in its most human form,
narrowing the space
between mortal and divine.

Broken Open

Tenderly,
tenderly
we tread on this soil,
tenderly,
tenderly,
we trample the seeds,
their hard shells pushed below,
out of sight,
preparing for the moment
when they dare to break through,
cracked open and vulnerable—
to creep out of dark soil
into the unknown—
their debut met
with a radiant nod,
tenderly,
tenderly,
they stretch into the light.

Museum of the Ordinary

I read that kids will spend
ninety-three percent of the time
they will ever spend
with their parents by the time
they finish high school.
Only a single digit of togetherness
left in the hourglass—

So let me take today,
set it under a cloche,
tag it in cursive,
and mount it on a shelf
where I can revisit it on afternoons
when the clank of the radiator
is the only sound in the house—
as dust motes settle
onto forgotten rock collections
and snow globes undisturbed.

Let me tag this unseasonable December day
that lured us out for lacrosse
in the backyard,
my daughter and I
slinging a ball through chilled air,
to jockey tufts of grass mid-thaw
and yelp at errant throws
sent rollicking into the street.

She stays outside—
and from the kitchen window
I see her fling the ball straight up,

face expectant and flushed
as a Titian goddess,
eyes fixed with a Kingfisher's gleam.
She plucks the target from the sky
with a sweeping arc
and streaks out of view.

These are the moments I'll catalogue,
a Dewey Decimal of a life lived together,
ordinary,
mundane,
and irretrievably ours.

The Profligate Universe

You are the pine tree,
the earthworm,
the spinning girl in the red dress.

I am the egret,
a gourd hanging off
a twisted vine,
the boy with a far-off stare.

They are the milkweed
and the monarch,
the moon
and the outgoing tide.

Together,
we are the crow,
the soil,
the dancing
of ancient stars
across a newborn sky.

Acknowledgments

Gratitude to the editors of the publications and websites where the following poems were first published and/or honored:

"A Visitation at Dinner:" Winner, Robert Frost Poetry Prize, Robert Frost Foundation

"The Sound of Two Hands Touching:" Shortlist, Jack Grapes Poetry Prize, *Cultural Review Weekly*

"Wire Monkey:" Winner, JuxtaProse Poetry Prize, *JuxtaProse Literary Review*

"Incoming:" *Missing Persons: Reflections on Dementia*, Beatlick Press

"Rest Here:" Finalist, New Millennium Writing Prize in Poetry

"Instinct:" Featured Reading, Harvard Reunion Memorial Service, *Memorial Hall Program*

"Baker's Secret:" Finalist, The Hal Prize, *Peninsula Pulse*

"Morning Fix:" Finalist, Joy Bale Boon Prize, *Heartland Review*

"Moving to the Uncanny Valley" & "Museum of the Ordinary:" Honorable Mention, Princemere Poetry Prize

"To the Brink:" Finalist, Rash Award for Poetry, *Broad River Review*

"The Muses:" Winner, Palm Beach Poetry Festival Competition

· · · · ·

With Gratitude

The writing of this collection coincided with some trying times: the descent of my mother into dementia and beyond, eternal Covid lockdowns, the emptying of our nest, an unwelcome diagnosis, and more. It almost didn't see the light of day but for the support of the crew in our little blue house.

To Rick & Rory, thank you for seeing me, supporting me, and calming me when the ghosts came out to play. Your belief in me is stitched into every page. I'm blessed by your grace and overwhelming capacity to love—even when my computer crashes...

To my friends in life and poetry, you make this solitary work bearable. Sharing the journey (and a glass of wine) with you is the best reward. I want more time with all of you. Deepest gratitude to: Maile & Rod, Kathryn & David, Sean M., Justen A., Amy B., Nancy & Rob, Katrina R., Martha F., Dana H., Susan H., Ann C., Tricia K., Kathy L., Jeff & Harry F., Mary F., Rebecca C., Beth P., Mitch N., Alyce t., the Andover Poet Laureate Committee, The Robert Frost Foundation, Dan & Emily + the ACT cohort, and my writing compadres from the Bread Loaf Writers' Conference, Prospect Street House, and Noepe Residencies.

To my siblings who have been there from the beginning, I wish us more laughter and adventures ahead.

And to you, dear poetry reader, I hope this book finds you well. My wish is that something in these pages might expand your joy or make your day a drop brighter. Thank you for taking this ride with me.

About the Author

Linda Flaherty Haltmaier is an award-winning author and Poet Laureate Emeritus of Andover, MA. Named the winner of the Robert Frost Poetry Prize, she is known for her "sensational imagery, her deft ear for the music in language, and her emotional sonar for sounding the depths of love (and anger.)" Her debut poetry collection, *Rolling up the Sky*, was awarded the Homebound Publications Poetry Prize and her follow-up collection, *To the Left of the Sun*, was named the winner of the International Book Award for Poetry. Additional accolades include winning the JuxtaProse Poetry Prize and the Palm Beach Poetry Festival Competition, as well as Finalist honors for the Princemere Poetry Prize, the New Millennium Award for Poetry, the Joy Bale Boone Poetry Prize, the Rash Award for Poetry, and the Tucson Festival of the Book Literary Award.

Her work has been nominated four times for the Pushcart Prize and featured widely in journals and anthologies including *WSQ, Cultural Review, Voices of the Sacred Wild*, and more. Her first chapbook, *Catch and Release*, was published by Finishing Line Press. A graduate of Harvard, Linda leads poetry workshops, gives readings, and promotes poetry on the North Shore of Boston where she lives with her husband and daughter. Her workshop, *Poetry & The Art of Noticing*, can be found at Living Whole Online.

You can find her at www.lindahaltmaier.com and on Instagram @linda.thepoet

Made in the USA
Las Vegas, NV
25 July 2024

92873859R00059